C000097616

ANNALS OF THE PO

And some there be that have no memorial

Too many people have been deterred from tracing their ancestors in the past by the fear that 'there won't be anything about them'. Others have been led to invent romantic tales because they think (a) they will never find the truth and (b) no one else will either. It is rash to assume that poor ancestors have left no documentary evidence behind them. In fact, the poorer they were, the more there is likely to be.

Back to 1837, everyone in England and Wales is, or should be, equally well documented at St Catherine's House and in the censuses. Before that, parish registers give details of poor residents as well as rich ones, and there is just as likely to be a personal comment about the appearance, habits and character of a poor man, especially in the burial register. Full details of these sources are given in other Guides in this series.

The parish poor

Before 1834, the parish itself was the normal unit of local government, administered by a collection of untrained officials, chosen
from among the local inhabitants and ratified by the local untrained
magistrates. The most important were the two Churchwardens, who saw
to the upkeep of church and churchyard, parish cottages, charities,
etc., and kept an eye on religious and moral welfare; and the two
Overseers, who looked after secular welfare in the parish, including
highways, bridges, watercourses, and the poor people.

Each parish was responsible for its own poor. There were five
basic classes of persons needing relief:
> the sick;
> the aged;
> widows, deserted wives and orphans;
> unemployed able-bodied inhabitants;
> destitute wanderers or temporary residents.

The sick were given nursing, not by trained nurses, but by village
women with aptitude and/or time; possibly medicine; and in extreme
cases, surgery, which tended to prove fatal equally for rich and poor.
Most illnesses ended rapidly in recovery or death, but a few men sur-
vived damaged, living in the parish for years, maimed or handicapped.
They were expected to do what they could to support themselves, but
might be given a small allowance, have their rent paid, and get
occasional hand-outs of bread and clothing from charity funds.

Widows who could do so were encouraged to support themselves, and
were sometimes given spinning wheels and a stock of wool as a starter.
Some did parish nursing or laundry work. Those with young children
got allowances and rent, but were encouraged to marry again or take
in actual orphans or the aged, for whom they were given allowances.

Orphans and widows' children were supported while small and their
allowance paid to whoever cared for them. Like other village children, they had to do whatever work they could from about 7, helping
about farms, watching livestock, etc. At about 14, they were apprenticed at the parish charge, sometimes to a craft, more often to
'husbandry' or 'domestic arts', meaning they were unpaid drudges in
farms or houses. Normal apprenticeships ended at 21, but parish ones
lasted until 24, giving the employer three more years of free service
for the cost of their keep. Some masters paid a little in the last
years, but it wasn't compulsory.

The aged were given an allowance, rent and nursing if need be, not
at a set age, but when they could no longer work. Finally, they would
be buried at the expense of the parish, which was not, at least in
the country, necessarily a cheap and undignified ending. A pauper
would, in a good parish, be decently coffined, borne and followed by
mourners, encouraged by a dole of bread and beer from the parish. It
was after 1834 that a 'pauper funeral' became such a bitter disgrace.

In some places there were almshouses (charity funded) which provided a comfortable last home for single or widowed aged. Applications

state age and length of residence and maybe other details - though few survive now.

All these classes of paupers might be given extra doles of clothing from time to time, from the Overseers or Churchwardens via charities.   Clothing was basic - shirts, shoes, shifts, the occasional waistcoat or coarse gown.   A poor apprentice was started off with a kit of clothes, then his master had to provide more as the lad grew, as necessary.

Able-bodied men who could find no work for the time were found a task about the parish.   Roads and bridges always needed repair and water-courses to be cleaned out.   Later, men were sent round ratepayers, who were obliged to find work for them for a number of hours. Men could not work in a craft to which they had not been apprenticed, but farming, haulage and general carrying was anyone's meat.   A craftsman fallen on evil times (by fire, say) might be lent money and expected to repay when he was on his feet again.   Only in general unemployment would an able-bodied man get an allowance, though his wife and children might be relieved if he was doing his best to help himself. Rent might be paid while a man was unemployed, though if he looked likely to be long-term, he might be moved into a 'parish house' kept for the purpose.

All details of the various allowances paid and why should be in the Overseers' Accounts for the parish, except for charitable grants, which were the affair of the Churchwardens.   The Churchwardens' Accounts list work done on the church, churchyard and parish houses and may name craftsmen and their labourers.   Not only wages but the amount spent on beer to wash down the plaster, etc., may be stated.

These account books were kept in the Parish Chest in the church when not in use, with Apprenticeship Indentures for poor children. Two copies were written of these on one sheet of parchment, cut across with a wavy or indented line.   The master kept one, the parish the other, till the full term was served.

Where did the money come from?

The money to provide the various allowances and to pay for parish financed works was then collected from the local inhabitants by the Overseers, according to the assessed value of their property, as with modern local rates. The Overseers had to calculate how much in total was likely to be needed, based on the previous years, but could call for a supplementary rate if sudden calamity occurred.   If this was specific to one village, aid might be sought from other parishes by sending a letter to be read out in church.   Collections 'for a Brief from So-and-so parish on account of the great Floode there' were made all over the country.   Some personal losses through fire and flood were the subject of Briefs, and they are sometimes listed in the backs of parish registers. This was a charity collection, not a fixed sum.

Because the Overseers were themselves ratepayers, they did not have the casual attitude to rate levies that modern paid officials have.   They spent no more than they had to, and sometimes pared down allowances to fit the money collected, rather than ask for more. Most parish overseers were just, if only because they knew that one day, they or their families might be a recipient, not a payer. It was reckoned fair to have the better-off members of the community pay to support men who had given good service to that community in their youth, or their widows and orphans. It was fair to help a man who was sick, or had a setback through misfortune. It was not at all fair to pay out good money to support someone who was too idle or too drunken to support himself. The Overseers knew all their clients and could apportion blame or show compassion with due regard for natural justice rather than the letter of the law. An aggrieved pauper could appeal, but most justices took the word of the Overseer.

It was regarded as totally unfair to have to support someone who didn't belong to the parish, but had come in and got into a situation which required relief. The stock of parish money was finite, and should go to parish folk. This was a very reasonable concept, which gave rise to a lot of misery in practice.

Settlement rules

In theory, each person had a 'place of settlement' where he belonged and was entitled to poor relief. It was simple enough for a man whose ancestors had always lived in the parish where he now resided. In time of trouble, the parish would cheerfully help - probably the Overseer was some sort of relative. It was when someone moved from a home parish that problems arose. If there were no jobs or houses, if he had made himself locally unpopular, if he was ambitious, a young man might decide to move. If he settled down, worked hard and behaved himself, he would progress upwards in the community, probably serve a parish office and, in age or want, have earned himself the right to support from the new parish. If things went wrong, he and his family were in trouble.

Up to 1662, a man could re-establish settlement by living in a new parish for three years. He might come in by invitation as a labourer for a farmer or tradesman, or, daringly, arrive and offer his services. This was risky, because spare houses would not be available. He could, if he had the nerve, build a small habitation on the Manor waste, as long as he could get it up and a fire going inside 24 hours. This needed co-operation, and implied he had friends and a job lined up already. Every house should have had four acres with it, so an undesirable could be evicted and his house pulled down on those grounds, if necessary.

The law was tightened up until in 1687, a man could be thrown out within 40 days of arrival, unless he had a house worth £10 a year (a large property). From 1691, he couldn't sneak over the boundary and lie low for 40 days, but must give notice of arrival, which was read out in church and written in a book, then wait 40 days. Most parishes threw out newcomers on principle, in case they should become poor or, worse, die leaving widow and orphans to the care of the parish. 'Here's a stranger, heave half a brick at him' was the rule, not a joke.

The normal ways in which a man could obtain or change his settlement were as follows:-

a. being born in a parish of a settled father;
b. paying taxes on a property in the parish;
c. serving as a parish officer (normally chosen from the ratepayers);
d. being apprenticed to a settled man for seven full years;
e. by being hired to work for a settled inhabitant for a complete year of 365 days.

The second and third implied money - and so less probability of needing relief. The fourth kind usually meant father had paid a premium. Some parishes aimed to apprentice their paupers - especially those from non-established families - outside the parish, to transfer the claim for future relief. A broken apprenticeship didn't count, so if the master died, that might be that, unless his relatives took over.

The last way was the common one by which a settlement was changed. Employers, as ratepayers, avoided casually adding to their own potential burden, by taking on men at one Hiring Fair and discharging them the day before the next. Until a man proved he was useful and healthy, he was never hired for the full year (actually a year and a day). It had to be continuous too - many a man had cause to regret asking a kind employer for a couple of days off for a family emergency. That broke his service.

Married men, especially those with children, were not allowed to resettle in this way. From 1697, they were permitted to come to a new village only if they could bring with them a Certificate of Settlement (see back cover) from their old parish, agreeing to take them back if they became chargeable to the rates. Tradesmen coming with a certificate could not bring their apprentices, who might thus become settled. 'Certificate men' only became settled when they started paying taxes or served a parish office.

If the non-settled man fell on evil times, he was sent back swiftly to his own parish. Certificate men were sent in a cart at the home parish's expense, which meant that most parishes would not issue a certificate for new homes over twenty miles or so away, over which removal costs became expensive. A man without a certificate might be dumped over the boundary to die in a ditch, especially if he was a wanderer from place unknown. For the ordinary labourer, the rule was that a Removal Order must first be obtained from a magistrate, and that this could be suspended if the person was sick. This rule was frequently broken.

A woman took her legal settlement from her husband, so if a man worked in a parish for years without gaining a settlement and married a local girl and died, his widow and children could be evicted from the only home they had ever known to a place where they were strangers. If the husband's family were not really local either and it just happened to be where he had once worked for 365 days, she wouldn't be very welcome. Some widows were set adrift to walk 'home' a few days after the husband's funeral.

The Examination of Benjamin Bishop of the Parish of Wendover in the County of Bucks Labourer concerning his place of legal settlement taken upon oath before me J. Junor, Clerk, one of his Majesty's Justices of the Peace in & for the said County this 29th day of Novr 1813 —

Who saith, that he believes he was born in the Parish of Williston in the County of Bucks, & that when he was about thirteen years of age he was hired by the week to Mr Gore of Tring in the County of Herts. as a Ploughboy at 4/6 p. week. Served him three years — He next hired himself to Mr Gregory in the Parish of Tring in the same County as a Servant in Husbandry for one year at the wages of 3..10..0 & at the expiration of that year, he hired himself again to the said Mr Gregory for another year at the wages of 4..0..0 — On leaving Mr Gregory's service, he hired himself to Mr Geary of Wendover in the County of Bucks for one year at 5..5..0 wages. After serving Mr Geary a year, he hired himself for a year to Mr Billington of Berkhampstead in the County of Herts, whom he served about 6 months, & was then drawn to serve in the Herts militia & served accordingly. After serving about three years in the Militia, he went to Sittingburn in the County of Kent, as a day Labourer, where he remained about twelve months, & then inlisted into the 15th Regt of Light Dragoons at Sittingburn. He served in that Regt 7½ years, & was then discharged in consequence of his wounds, & was sent to Garrison duty in the Tower in London, where he served rather more than a year, he was then discharged, & went again to day labor at Chelsea where he continued about 4 years; he then went to a haymaking about Enfield & returned to Wendover about six weeks since — This Examinant further saith, he does not know that he has done any act since he left the service of Mr Geary in Wendover, whereby he has gained a Settlement elsewhere —

Sworn before me
J. Junor, Clerk

the mark of ✕ Benjamin Bishop

An Examination as to Settlement, 1813.

Legally, a Removal Order had to be obtained, but these were often challenged, where the man's links with his parish of settlement were tenuous. Getting an order was complicated. First there was an 'Examination as to Settlement' which may state a man's birthplace and parentage and his career to when he arrived in the parish, with names of employers, wages and duration of service. The better the claim, the less detail. To avoid complications after a death, the Overseers tended to examine anyone who looked like becoming chargeable - a bad cold aroused suspicions. A really awkward case would be challenged by the 'home' parish which might adduce details of the father's and grandfather's settlement. Sometimes a parish paid out more in legal fees fighting a claim for settlement than it would have cost to keep a whole family for years.

The settlement parish could pay over the sum due for relief and leave the man or family where they were, if the new parish agreed. In this case, the payment out will be entered in the accounts of the home parish - a useful proof of connections over a distance.

Removal Orders and Examinations as to Settlement would also have been kept in the parish chest originally, and were carefully preserved lest the same man or family should try to re-enter the parish. To go through the legal process twice would have been very costly. Short details of the case will be found in the Quarter Sessions Records, if the parishes fought about a Settlement.

Bastards

Bastards were a special case, in that they were deemed to belong to the parish where they were born. This meant that a mother often did better not to marry a non-settled man and risk being ejected with him. A non-belonging girl, however, was thrown out as soon as her condition was suspected, sometimes on a trumped up charge of theft. If her settlement was known, she was sent there under a Removal Order. If she was a vagrant, she might be dumped in a ditch over the border just in time. However, there was an arrangement for the parish to get the money laid out on confinement and support back from the man, if they could catch him, and some parishes were very persistent in bringing the man back and making him marry the girl. Some rather devious Overseers would persuade an elderly pauper from another parish to marry a young expectant mother, thus shifting the cost elsewhere and striking a blow for morality at the same time.

Full details of the process are given in the Guide *Illegitimacy*, but, briefly, the girl was asked to name the man, and he was summoned to appear before the Overseers, or, if recalcitrant, the local magistrate. He could marry the girl; he could admit paternity and sign a Bastardy Bond, to pay for the confinement and maintenance. If he had no money, his parish or relatives might be asked to pay. Or he could pay the money at once. All the papers - over twenty printed forms - were in the parish chest originally.

If a man absconded, he might be pursued, apprehended and sent for trial locally or at the Quarter Sessions. The evidence in the case appears in the Sessions Rolls but a summary would be noted on parish forms, with the result of the case. This was almost always that the man had to sign the Bastardy Bond and pay up, with a possible period in gaol if he argued. The defence to the charge may add a new dimension to the ancestral character. Normally, the child's exact date of birth and sex is given in the Court record, but not the name. The occasional clever girl would swear her baby's father was the squire's son, when it was far more likely to have been a poor labourer, to finance a marriage which would not otherwise be possible, but there was usually some jealous person who gave her away, unless the squire was so unpopular that this was reckoned fair enterprise.

One way of avoiding having to pay up even if the responsibility wasn't in dispute was by joining the Army or Navy - and repetitive bastard-getters or petty criminals were encouraged to do so, for the good of their local Overseers' accounts. Service men could not be charged - though names of regiments and captains will be recorded to discourage desertion.

Where are they now?

All these papers from the parish chest may still be there, or may have been destroyed when no longer current, or given away as salvage in wartime. Some parchments were reused for Bishop's Transcripts if the backs were clean, or to stiffen book covers. Many have been deposited in County Record Offices and others trickle in still from time to time. Those still in churches, often in unlocked chests, are at risk from vandals or souvenir hunters.

Occasionally, an account book is in private hands, where the Overseer served frequently and came to regard the book as his own. Descendants will sometimes deposit, if they are told what the old things are.

Even when the Accounts are fragmentary or lost, a knowledge of the system will help to estimate what is probable. The settlement system was a brake on the mobility of labour among ordinary families and it restricted the range of movement. Craftsmen could move more easily and single men were more mobile than families.

The country labourer

The countryman had certain practical advantages over the towndweller. Even if his cottage lacked the legal four acres, he probably had a large garden, where he could grow vegetables and keep hens and a pig or two. Pre-enclosure, he also had certain rights over village common land, of grazing a cow, sheep, geese, etc., of collecting dead wood or turf where customary, and acorns and beechmast from the woods for his pigs, and the odd rabbit for the pot. Village women and children were allowed to glean or leaze - to gather up the fallen ears of corn after harvest - and the family could live well and even have a little surplus for sale in a good year.

Farm wages were fixed by the Justices, and fixed low, but only the beginner was restricted to these and he mostly lived in at the farm, so got food and keep. The householder was part self-supporting, part wage-earner - and these increased if he was any good.   When the old open-field cultivation system ended, so did common rights. Enclosures allowed farmers to fence off blocks of land and asserted the right of the lord of the manor to all commons.

The cottagers lost common rights and therefore could not keep large animals.   They were forced to rely more on wages, so the lowness mattered. Much free food was lost, for themselves and their animals, so was free wood for firing.   Women gleaning were accused of theft, since the farmers wanted to fatten their own hogs on the corn fallen. More and more men who had been part-time workers now competed for jobs.   In enclosed villages, distress was great by the 1790s and men fled to still open villages, placing a great strain on them.   There was a war on, and prices were rising rapidly, so even the wealthy noticed the desperate poverty to which farm labourers had fallen. Philanthropists tried to do something about it and even officials like magistrates decided that something should be done, if only to safeguard themselves from an English Revolution, like the one across the Channel.

The Speenhamland System

In 1795, a group of magistrates met in an inn parlour at Speenham-land, Berkshire, with the declared aim of fixing higher wages. Several drinks later, they ended by suggesting a rise plus free potatoes and fuel, but fixing merely the minimum rate at which parish allowances were paid.   This was to reflect the price of a gallon loaf.   A man could have the equivalent of three loaves a week, women and children one and a half each. This minimum was speedily adopted as a maximum, instead of any wage increase, and later pared down.

Each parish had its own system for coping with able-bodied poor. Some collected more money or set them on parish work, but numbers increased with new enclosures.   Most settled for the new 'roundsman' system.   A poor unemployed man had to go round the local tradesmen · and farmers till he found one to offer work.   Ratepayers had to employ them - which pressed heavily on the craftsman who could not use unskilled labour and the small farmer, managing with the help of his sons, who could not afford outside labour. Some of these were ruined and joined the ranks of the poor.

The large farmers liked the idea, because they paid half wages and the parish the rest, making it up to Speenhamland levels.   Some farmers dismissed their regular workers and used roundsmen only.   A really cunning man employed men from the next village, so he didn't have to pay rates as a contribution.

The roundsman system was degrading, with workmen always begging for the chance to work.   It increased the gap between rich and poor, but at least it kept men at home, and in work some of the time.   In some places, old-established farmers tried to keep on their old work-men, and increased demand for produce during the war helped to absorb some extra labour.

Then the war ended and with it the artificial prosperity. Imports competed for markets and there was a series of bad harvests, partly caused by over-cropping in the days of high demand, and a failure to rest or fertilise the newly enclosed fields. The old system may not have been efficient, but at least it allowed land to rest and running livestock on it helped to fertilise it naturally.

This ruined more farmers – often the better-natured ones, with long-established local connections and poor relatives among the workers. It let into the countryside a new class of 'money-men' – war-profiteers and City merchants, who bought up country estates and tried to run them like counting houses.

The moneymen slashed the Speenhamland allowances to the bone – to two loaves a week – and rejected the sensible suggestion of providing land allotments for the poor to rent to support themselves. They treated the grumblings caused by malnutrition and real distress as revolutionary infection from France. They also introduced machinery into farming, since it speeded work and needed no food. This increased unemployment and when desperate men burnt ricks, stole turnips and broke machinery, this was proof of political sedition. As the money-men had become magistrates too (which went with owning the 'Big House') they were able to punish the poor savagely.

Crime

Increasingly, the records of the poor are the records of crime. A poor man had only to step a little out of line to be severely punished. Claiming old common rights resulted in punishment for gleaning (by criminal grannies) or picking up dead wood and beechmast. Snaring rabbits was worse than stealing turnips, since it spoilt the fun of gentlemen who wanted rough shooting. Organised demonstrations against machinery in 1830, called 'Captain Swing' riots, after the mythical leader, were savagely repressed, and 400 men were transported to Australia for life. Many men died in an attempt to poach rabbits or game, for the keepers set lethal spring guns on paths and in coppices. This did not count as murder, though attacking keepers did. The choice was often a straightforward one between starvation and crime. Many of the 'criminals' were only doing what their ancestors had done as of right, with the added incentive that they were now poaching to save their families from starvation. They felt they had more right to the wild produce than incoming strangers, even if these men had bought the manor house and park.

Apart from semi-political crimes – which would now come under the umbrella of legitimate trade-union activity, the poor were inevitably more likely to figure in normal crime statistics. Although they were not necessarily more criminal than the rich, they had more reason to commit crimes and far more chance of being found out and punished. Court records of any period are worth checking for a reference to a poor ancestor. Indeed, the only ancestors who are easy to trace before parish registers – apart from property owners – are criminals. You may give thanks for coming of a long line of horse thieves.

At all stages from the sixteenth century, justice was dispensed locally by untrained magistrates (J.Ps.) often sitting informally in their own houses, and by the King's judges, who travelled on circuit round the country. They visited county towns about four times a year, and the records are preserved in the Quarter Sessions rolls. They dealt with a ragbag of offences, from failure to repair roads and bridges by way of bastardy and settlement cases to murder and theft. Some rolls have been abstracted and printed, or unpublished calendars may be available in County Record Offices.

A complete list, county by county, for England and Wales, of years covered and the extent of calendars and indexes, etc., is in the FFHS Guide to *Quarter Sessions Records for Family Historians*.

The volumes are huge (or are still in rolls) and ease of reading varies according to period. The case will be referred to several times, from the indictment onwards. The jury may find a 'True Bill' or case to answer, in which case, it went to trial. The accused may be remanded on bond to appear later, or be kept in gaol. A bond had to be backed by two guarantors, often relatives or friends from the home village, which helps if the crime is committed elsewhere, since it is the location of the crime which is stated in the indictment. (The accused is usually described as of that place, as he had at least briefly been so at the time of the crime. If he was described as of somewhere else, and that could be shown to be wrong, then the case could fail.) The witnesses also had to swear bonds to appear and their guarantors may be useful also (for those who dislike the idea of finding their ancestors accused of crime, remember they may figure as the injured parties or as witnesses).

Some cases hang on from session to session and then fizzle out – probably because the accused had had lawyers or friends working behind the scenes on his behalf. Also in the days before a professional police force, prosecution of crime and administration of justice was haphazard and inefficient.

Both charges and sentences may seem peculiar to modern eyes. Stealing a handkerchief or a rusty horseshoe may be punished by transportation, whereas assault and battery on a tax collector rated a sixpenny fine. A great deal depended on the status and friendships of the accused and the personal inclinations of the judge that day. The lower courts are even less consistent. Theft of property worth more than 40 shillings was a hanging matter, which accounts for the merciful alteration of value to 39 shillings 11 pence. Personal vendettas and prejudice played a great part, so a poaching fine may be followed by window breaking at the informant's home, and an uppity labourer whose real crime was agitation for better wages may be framed on a charge of theft to get rid of him.

Letters by the judge or diaries of local gentry, or careful investigation done as a university thesis may have since been published or deposited at the local C.R.O. This could show the reason for a really odd decision. Sometimes a bout of indigestion or a hangover may be the only cause of unusually severe punishment for a trivial crime.

The poor in the towns

Very large towns, of which there were few before 1850, were special cases in regard to settlements, and the way in which they dealt with the poor.   London, Sheffield, Birmingham, Manchester, Bristol and a few others were large enough to be anonymous. Men could go there on speculation, with a very good chance of finding a job within a day or two, provided they were adaptable and did not have ideas of setting up for themselves in a craft trade, in competition with the City fathers.   The rule that only apprenticed men could trade in a craft was intensified in London to mean only a locally apprenticed one, though a fully qualified provincial could buy his way into a local trade guild or company if he had enough money and a friend at court. This was not open to a poor man, who had to depend on finding an employer.

Towns could absorb any number of strong young men (and even women). There was no place for the weak or sick or aged, however. A man could work till he died of industrial disease or the fevers which ravaged the mean streets.   If he recovered but was too ill to work, he might try to stagger back 'home' or be sent there, for it was very difficult indeed to get a settlement in a town, and no certificates were issued to let the men move elsewhere. One alternative for able-bodied labourers who had failed in one town was to try another - so the main roads were thronged with travellers trying their luck.

The large towns, and even some smaller ones, were run by a Mayor and burgesses, not parish elders, though they called themselves 'the Vestry'.   Little lip service was paid to the religious duty of suc-couring the poor and needy.   It was something which had to be done, to keep untidy heaps of beggars and dying off the streets. There was little sense of community for all classes in the place. Many labourers were newcomers who had come seeking work and fortune and failed to make it.   There were few really old local families among the poor - people got on or got out.   Some of the employers operated a sort of benevolent scheme for their own men, but for most, the security net was full of holes.

Workhouses

Towns rarely gave out-relief (leaving paupers in their own houses and paying rent and allowances). They preferred to eject their poor and pack them into purpose-built workhouses, after 1722 (earlier in London). The system was to appoint a Workhouse Master and leave him to administer the poor. He had a certain amount to spend on food, so he aimed to keep down the number of paupers sharing it.   He failed to provide nursing for the sick, turned pregnant girls out into the snow and kept the poor on such inadequate rations that they died fast of starvation.   Because town workhouses took in not only the sick, mad and pregnant, but also able-bodied men and their families, an alternative name was the House of Industry.   The poor had to earn their keep - or, precisely, to add to the profit.   Stocks of wool, leather and metal, etc., were provided and the inmates set on producing goods, sold for the profit of the Master and Vestry. Sometimes the workhouse did sub-contract work for local mills, sometimes the products were sent to rival towns to undercut prices there. At least this was better than picking oakum, a gaol punishment also used in some country workhouses to keep the able-bodied out of mischief.

Because extra paupers meant more useless mouths to feed, the Master segregated males and females. If a girl came in pregnant, she and her infant stood a good chance of dying. Only if a girl caught the eye of the Master was she likely to get pregnant after arrival. Division of the sexes broke up many hitherto happy families, for the men deserted from the workhouse and ran off alone, leaving their families to suffer.

Some workhouses have surviving records listing inmates, which give date and place of birth, occupation, reason for entry plus career in the workhouse. Other books listed diet and clothing and possibly work done and profits - though the workhouse masters tended to play it close to the chest. Often these records were destroyed, since they gave away too much. If they exist, they should now be in county or town archives. Some of the worst cases of abuse were brought to public attention and investigated, in which case there may (at least in the nineteenth century) be a newspaper report.

The New Poor Law

In 1834, control of relief of the poor was taken away from the parish and transferred to the Union, which was a group of six, a dozen or more parishes, according to size. Control was in the hands of a Board of Guardians, chosen from local gentry, clergy and major tradesmen, in most cases not even remotely related to or familiar with the paupers they were asked to relieve. They were thus inclined to look after the interests of the ratepayers entirely, not the paupers. Poverty now was regarded very much as somehow the fault of the poor person - even somewhat of a crime to be punished by harsh treatment. The Board could never imagine the day when their families or themselves would be paupers, so they did not mind establishing a precedent of harsh treatment. Workhouses had been spreading gradually to most medium-sized towns, especially those on main roads, and now every Union built at least one. Out-relief was almost abolished and some poor who would otherwise have been only temporary paupers, had their rent been paid for a few weeks, were forced to break up their homes and move into the 'House' or forego relief. The normal thing for a pauper, without relatives who could or would help, was the Workhouse. Hard work and short commons were all that an aged labourer could look forward to, and the sheer disgrace of ending in the Workhouse was enough to kill off many paupers rapidly.

The vestiges of the settlement system still operated and any poor who could be said to belong to someone else were sent back to their own Union Workhouse as soon as the magistrates' order could be obtained. As certificates had been abolished, many poor persons had no sure 'home' Union, but might be shunted to and fro while legal wrangles continued. Relatives were not allowed to take in pauper children unless they could indemnify the parish, which only the better-off could do.

One of the added bitternesses attached to workhouse life was that most of the poor had to wear a sort of uniform, a coarse gown or cotton suit, sometimes with 'P' for pauper and a letter for the name of the parish. Their own clothing and any small possessions were taken from them on entrance. If they ran away from the intolerable House, they had stolen the uniform. The sexes were separated, and old couples of fifty years standing ended their days apart, enduring the last indignities among strangers.

Records of this period should also be found in county or town archives, but Minutes of the Board of Guardians tend to concern themselves with self-congratulations, not details of paupers. They are most useful when an attempt was made to force a distant relative to pay for pauper support, since the addresses of known relations are recorded, with their replies to the demands. This covers a period of general migration from country to town.

Rogues, vagabonds and sturdy beggars

Anathema to the parish authorities were the folk who wandered the country with no settlement or any wish for one and no visible means of support. They were lumped together as 'rogues, vagabonds and sturdy beggars' and it was permissible to eject them or throw them in the village lock-up, at will.

Naturally, some were wandering bands of thieves, ready to steal anything which wasn't nailed down and to con the locals out of food and money with hard luck stories. Some of the beggars painted on or self-inflicted wounds or ulcers, which they swore they got in the wars, though mainly did their act in towns or at fairs, where the audience was large. There is little record of these men, since they rarely left cards.

Companies of actors and circus type performers also travelled round the country in carts. The only early theatres were in London, and provincial performances were in barns or inns or from carts. If one of the family was successful, the history of the rest may have been collected (as with the Kembles and Robertsons), but for the run-of-the-mill performer, information is hard to find. One snag is that some were from respectable families, even gentry, so used false names.

Poor persons making a journey sometimes walked great distances for work or to get home to their parish. Some were taken up as criminals (if they picked a handful of wayside fruit, say) but, on the whole, if they looked respectable and were not sick or pregnant, they could shelter in a barn overnight and even get a few pence to speed them on their way. Some had an official pass which said where they were going and why, so were designated 'passengers' or 'waygoers'. If they did fall ill, they might be allowed to stay, but if they died or gave birth, the parish register would note the settlement place, to avoid future claims for settlement (and recover funeral charges, if possible).

Some clergy were better than others at discovering and recording details - some just note 'a stranger' or 'a wayfaring child'.

'Travellers' in parish registers often means gipsies or other semi-permanent itinerants. Proper gipsies subsisted by fortune telling, circus tricks and - mainly - by selling horses, which they sometimes bought, sometimes stole. They covered a wide area of country to avoid retribution.

Others classed as gipsies were really travelling tradesmen, the Hoover mechanics of their day, who acted as tinkers or general metal workers. They went from village to village in carts, at fairly regular intervals, mending pots, pans, and the small mechanisms, including clocks. They travelled within a limited area, each family apparently having a 'territory' which was their own to work. Once established, they can readily be traced by a blanket search of all parishes in it, since they mostly were regular baptisers. Their names were often exotic, through mixing with travelling troupes of actors and hearing plays rehearsed.

Very similar were pedlars, hucksters and higglers, who took packs of small goods out to villages, or went round buying small manufactures for resale. They had set areas to work and needed licences to trade, so were known as 'badgers', from the licence badge worn. On a grander scale were chapman, who worked the towns with sample packs of goods, and supplied customers from warehouses in one town. Few of these took families with them, but often found wives in distant places, so might re-visit.

All wanderers were treated with suspicion, but those who worked the same villages regularly were accepted as providing a useful service. Their 'poverty' was doubtful, for they would not advertise that they carried much money in their carts.

Soldiers were similarly mobile and some took their families with them. If regiment or officer is named in the parish register, you can find other towns where the family is likely to have gone, and even trace the original marriage to a girl from a far distant county. Army records may help trace the origins of soldiers who settle down where their brides came from, after leaving the army.

Official reports

Whenever poverty became a national issue, there were official persons and bodies who reported on it. Most of these reports of official commissions were published as Parliamentary papers and many contain a wealth of detail about the individuals called upon to give evidence. Every problem which became the subject for legislation - parish apprentices, poor relief allowances, children in the mines, factory conditions - had a Royal Commission report, and all are worth reading for background information, and the chance to finding actual ancestral gold. Hansard, the reports of parliamentary proceedings, also contains speeches with personal details about constituents' problems, among a great deal of waffle about foreign policy and religious dogma. Organised migration schemes from rural to industrial areas produced official lists.

During most of the nineteenth century, private gentlemen and journalists were collecting evidence about the problems of the poor and much of it was published. There is a useful list of books and articles in *The Town Labourer* and *The Village Labourer* by J.L. and Barbara Hammond. Among contemporary sources are William Cobbett's *Political Register* and *Rural Rides* (early 19th century); Henry Mayhew's *London Labour and the London Poor* (1851); Friedrich Engels' *Condition of the Working Classes in England* (1844, Manchester and Sheffield); and the Reports of the Society for Bettering the Conditions of the Poor (1795-1808). A good rummage in libraries will often produce something relevant to your ancestral area or trade.

When is a pauper not a pauper?

The fact that a man signed his name with a cross doesn't prove he was a pauper. Many farmers could not write and even gentlemen were not facile sometimes. Unless there was a village schoolmaster, fathers might not bother to educate their sons, still less their daughters. After 1870, all children should have gone to school, but some slipped the net.

For a few years from 1783, register entries of baptisms and burials may have 'pd 3d' or 'P' against them. 'P' meant pauper. The clergy had been ordered to collect a tax on entries and forward it to the government, unless the person was a pauper. They resented the work, so to frustrate the tax man, overnight, everyone not paying land tax would be offered the 'P' designation - and most took it happily.

A somewhat similar situation occurred over a century earlier, in the lists of payers of Hearth Tax. All householders were assessed, but paupers were excused paying. Some managed to avoid paying by getting themselves categorised as paupers when other sources suggest they were reasonably well-off - but friends with the assessors. In the 1660s some county lists (arranged by parish) specifically list those excused payment, and in the early 1670s there were printed forms for this purpose. The FFHS Guide to *The Hearth Tax, Other Later Stuart Tax Lists and the Association Oath Rolls* lists the surviving documents, their location (mostly in the Public Record Office, Chancery Lane, London) and transcripts or indexes.

The poor are always with us?

A family which was poor in the nineteenth century may have been ruined by the enclosures which did for the small farmers. It is always worth looking for wills further back, when they were affluent. Don't be put off by finding ag. labs. wall to wall in the census. Some labourers then went to the factories or worked on the railways and struck it rich late last century - so don't imagine that comfortable incomes for the last two or three generations mean the family were never poor. Chance, good or bad health, hard work or laziness could alter the social status any time. There are no tight compartments for classes in Britain. Most people's ancestry is a splendid mixture of rich and poor, upper class and labourers.